HOW TO BE A NIGERIAN

How to be

a

NIGERIAN

by

PETER ENAHORO

Drawings by Chucks Anyanwu

Printed in Nigeria by
The Caxton Press (West Africa) Limited, Ibadan

FOR REMI

"Though tribe and tongue may differ
In brotherhood we stand,
Nigerians all. . ."

—From the National Anthem.

HOW TO BE
A
NIGERIAN

A guide book for natives and expatriates on the conduct, deportment, comportment, bearing, demeanour, mien, carriage, air, port, actions; the misdoings, misconduct and misbehaviours of the Nigerian adult male and female.

by
Peter Enahoro

CONTENTS

PREAMBLE

It is not easy to write a book. First, you have to get a book; then you have to write it. That has been my experience.

I did not set out to write a book when I began putting notes down about the Nigerian. It just struck me one day that with all the political acrimony that gripped the country and in spite of the diversity of the country, a personality that was distinctly "Nigerian" had emerged, but few Nigerians realised it.

One night, sitting in front of the Catering Rest House bungalow in Maiduguri, almost a thousand miles from Lagos, I was talking this matter over with a German journalist friend, Lutz Herold, * when he suggested it might be a good idea to put my views down in a book. I protested at once and made charges against myself that I was not the authc -type. Lutz refused to yield and since I am succeptible to flattery, I finally allowed myself to be persuaded. I hope this book is a success.

It is very important that people should be told how to be a Nigerian. Apart from the fact that Nigerians themselves will be most interested, every fifth African in this Continent, is a Nigerian. We are talking therefore of about a quarter of the people of this Continent. Too many writers are trying to solve Africa's political and economic problems without looking at the people with whom they are dealing. Others, with less concern for the immediate problems, worry their heads sore abo.it the "tragic impact of European influence". We are be-deviled by over-anxious curators of culture who lament the

---

* Lutz Herold was the free-lance journalist jailed 40 years by Nkrumah's regime in Ghana, for "misimprison of treason". He was released after the Army revolt of February 24, 1966, and returned to Europe.

fact that Africa is no longer the primitive continent they dreamed it to be.

I anticipate furor in quarters which have become accustomed to the fawnings of the European psycophant. Such people are bound to see_this book as an "insult" to the Nigerian. I offer no apologies.

I offer this book as a tourist guide to those Nigerians who wish to break with tradition and visit their own country. Nigerians are great travellers, except in their own country. They travel far and wide in Africa. You will find them selling diamonds to Ivoriens in Ivory Coast; they run small businesses in Ghana and make a thundering good living selling hand-woven Ghanaian cloth to Ghanaians. You will find them in the heart of the Congo too, selling elephant tusks off Congolese elephants to the Congolese. But at home they are parochial. Flatterers say we are a stable people. No doubt about that. At home, the Nigerian is intrinsically static. They are stable people who are immobile.

This book does not pretend that it is a philosophical or sociological work; it does not affect to be of scholarly depth. Its aim is to enlighten in an entertaining way, to show that the Nigerian can laugh at his own idiosyncracies.

For this reason, I commend this book to the man with a large sense of humour.

Lagos, 1966.   Peter Enahoro.

WHO ARE THE NIGERIANS?

The search for the Nigerian is in progress.

Optimists say that before this century is out, the experiment begun in the 19th century will produce such a people.

Meanwhile, there are Hausas, Yorubas, Tivs, Edos, Fulanis, Ibos and 87 other lesser peoples inhabiting that area of geography bordered by the Republics of Cameroun, Chad, Niger and Dahomey, in an area of 378,000 square miles, which is four times the size of Great Britain.

There are 55.6 million Nigerians. Perhaps another two million live abroad, scattered throughout Africa.

History records that several hundred years ago a band of European adventurers found a route through the Cape of Good Hope to India where the Trade Winds had driven them. It was the Age of Discovery.

The traders were soon followed by pirates who formed labour recruitment agencies for the farms of the New World. At first they came in trickles as raiders to plunder and pillage, carting off sardine packages of slaves to America.

Each European state that had the naval might and the sailors' mettle to dare the voyage fitted out a boat and came to transport human cargoes for sale in God's Own Country.

Eventually something had to be done about Africa, for the African chieftains (middle-men between the producers of human merchandise and consumers of slavery) were constantly warring among themselves, wasting the precious produce in the process and disrupting the flow of trade.

The good people of Europe decided that this threat to their economy could not be tolerated much longer.

Fired by this zeal, a conference was summoned for Berlin; agenda, the compulsory liquidation of existing tribal empires and the arbitrary delimitation of the continent of Africa into puppet states. This way, Africa would be assigned to the care of European powers. Civilisation was born. It was all so noble!

At the conference which was convened in 1884, the British representative stood up and pointing to a crude map, declared: "Gentlemen, the Hottentots and Bantu Negroes in this part of West Africa will be protected by us henceforth."

The French made a throaty bid over large areas in the same territory; the Spaniards, long dissipated and the Portuguese, half forgotten, both said something that sounded like protest, but their voices were faint and Mr. Chairman gavelled the Briton's bid.

The area under reference went to Her Brittanic Majesty, Queen Victoria, Empress of India.

In keeping with their promise to keep safe, defend and guard the "Protectorate of Nigeria," the British unfurled the Union Jack, set up trading posts and called in missionaries from Scotland to preach the gospel of liberty. Thus, was Nigeria born.

There were still bush-fire rebellions to snuff out before the total submission of the natives was achieved. History books call them "expeditions." They are obviously not landmarks because British forces did not expend much ammunition in the campaigns and the Exchequer had no cause for alarm.

Today, the conglomeration of tribes assembled compulsorily at the 1884 Berlin conference are assigned as Nigerians—for want of a substitute collective noun.

2

UNITY IN DIVERSITY

Europeans talk about the weather; *Nigerians talk about tribe*.

The Nigerian society is strictly organised into a variety of tribes. So consuming is the devotion to tribe that if St. Peter were a Nigerian, four-fifths of us would be wasting our time in church and Heaven would soon spill out The Gatekeeper's tribal group of Nigerians.

Tribes transcends individuality.

You would hear one Nigerian describing another Nigerian to a third Nigerian. If the third Nigerian is at sea and does not know to whom his informant is referring, the first Nigerian would then bring him ashore with: "I am talking about that Yoruba man."

There are 13,000,000 Yorubas and what this amounts to is like trying to identify a pebble in a sand-bank.

But the reference to his tribe already points to the kind of man he is *certain* to be. The gentleman in question may never be known by name throughout the conversation, but the fact that he is Yoruba, or Ibo, or Efik is sufficient to identify him.

Not only is his social, political and economic outlook determined immediately, even his possible reaction to a given situation, his secret thoughts, are reasonably suspected on the understanding that members of the same tribe are all alike!

No one knows how effective this sytem of mental "Identikit" is for long-range screening better than employers, hospitals and the churches who ask you to give your tribe on your church subscription card. Doctors cannot cure you of fresh colds unless they know to what tribe you belong. Until this day when filling your application forms you are dared to state your

3

'They're all alike...'

tribe, but never your nationality.

This does not mean that a European necessarily will get a job faster than a Nigerian. But it means that a Togolese or the Afro-American who can lose his accent, has a rosier opportunity provided he is not squeamish about his tribal origin back home.

All members of a tribe are brothers.

This feeling of close affinity in the tribe is more than fraternal sentiment. It fills the place of employment agency.

If you say to your cook, "I want a reliable steward," he will promise to bring you his brother who has just arrived from their home town and is temporarily sharing a bed with another brother in the farthest corner of town.

That evening, your cook will slip out and despatch a telegram.

Two days later, he will introduce his brother to you, but it will be many months before you are allowed into the knowledge that his "brother" is, as the expression goes, merely "my town's man."

"I sent for him from home," your cook will say unabashed and with a glint of satisfaction in his eyes. If you ask him why he told you they were brothers, he will insist that they are brothers.

Tribal groups organise private co-operative societies which impose tolls on members and build schools, maternity hospitals, churches and send "brothers" abroad to study degree courses.

Appropriately, tribal unions are named to show their particular programmes. Thus you have "Ishakole Improvement Union." This means that the Ishakole area has been developed but requires improvement. "Nosaya Development Association." This is a charge of negligence on the part of Government, which can then be seen as having failed to develop the Nosaya area. "The Izobo Progressive Union," reveals that the Izobos are developed, do not seek improvement but progress.

Sometimes a tribe is united in rebellion against the authorities and you have an intimidating title as: "Ikara United Taxpayers Association."

These unions are feared by politicians and it became the custom in the First Republic to court their support by reciting the vote-catching slogan, "our unity is in our diversity." This was repeated for the umpteenth time but it never failed to draw cheers. In fact, if a politician said nothing more for the duration of his electioneering, he was still praised for his sharp intellect, remarkable foresight and patriotism.

At all times the Nigerian blames his tribe for his bad fortune, his poor education, lack of promotion, car accident, penury, sickness and failure to raise an overdraft from a British bank.

Never agree with him. Or disagree.

If you agree with him, you are fanning the embers of tribalism by suggesting that something is wrong with his tribe. If you disagree with him, you are not facing up to facts and Nigerian unity can never be achieved by running away from the sceptre of tribalism.

THE CHAIRMAN

Next to God, there is nothing that fills the heart of the Nigerian with greater awe than a Chairman.

God is divine, but the Chairman rules the temporal. In certain parts of Nigeria, the office of Prime Minister can only be understood if you explain that he is the Chairman of the Government.

A Chairman is appointed to direct a lecture. There is a Chairman at a football match, a wedding reception, a naming ceremony, funeral, political rallies and benefit film shows. Such is the passion that if three cub-scouts are lost in the woods, they will very likely appoint a Chairman to lead them safely back to the wolf pack.

What qualifies a man for selection as Chairman has never been clearly defined. He may be a wealthy member of the community. On the other hand, he may be a washed-up but gravely dignified bankrupt. Or, a contributing columnist whose articles in the Press are outstanding because no one understands them.

All experienced Chairmen have a sense of showmanship.

Not only is he expected to distinguish himself in sartorial flamboyance, he carries a bundle of files and has a younger relative or servant trailing behind him, bearing an umbrella.

The umbrella is a status symbol and only men of culture and distinction may carry umbrellas in the dry season. The umbrella also falls handy if in the midst of heated argument, the Chairman is compelled to mete out discipline.

Long before the event over which he is to preside, the practised Chairman would spend hours before the mirror,

Where two or more are gathered...

improvising, gesticulating and polishing up his accent so that when he does make his speech, he has everyone confounded. People are accustomed to not understanding their Chairman and they will form a most excellent impression if he speaks between clenched teeth.

The Chairman is ushered to the platform after an elaborate introduction which has its set pattern of protocol. It begins with the m.c. seeking attention but is held up in a traffic jam of interruptions as everybody turns to hush-up everybody else.

Protocol demands that the m.c. keeps the name of the Chairman a closely guarded secret until the tail end of the introduction when he may offer it as the highlight of his speech. Although the name has been published in the programme, in handbills and on posters, this stunt is welcomed with joyous approval.

The m.c. says that it is his bounden duty, his responsibility, his pride and pleasure "to introduce our father for this evening's occasion."

"Everyone knows that there cannot be two Chairmen for the same occasion (*cheers*). Therefore, we can only pick one captain for our boat tonight (*prolonged applause*). We all know the man I have in mind but before I call upon him to assume the chair, I will seek your indulgence and his kind permission to digress a little.

"Who is this man who will be our Chairman this evening? He studied London matriculation in Bombay after the war, having retired from the RAF as a full sergeant (*loud ovation*).

"He did not return home, but went to London to seek the golden fleece (*a sigh of admiration permeates the audience*). He struggled on without a town union support or government scholarship until he passed his B.A. and his intermediate LL.B. (*prolonged loud ovation*).

"Since returning home, our august Chairman tonight has been personally responsible for drafting four petitions to

9

Government concerning the improvement of social amenities in our town in particular and Nigeria in general." (*Standing ovation*).

The Chairman-elect rises and strides purposedly to the platform. He bows solemnly and commences: "Ladies and gentlemen, when I was apprised of the invitation to chairman this occasion, I perceived that there were many better qualified than myself."

The audience is not deeply touched by this humility, although they would sneer if he did not take time off from the main proceedings to humble himself in this manner. Everyone knows that Mr. Chairman is only making the customary opening gambit and that what he really means is that no one present is better qualified to be Chairman than himself.

With calculated insinuation the Chairman launches a sly attack on his social rivals. By insisting that he had only half-heartedly accepted to be Chairman, he unmasks other outstanding figures in the community whose image and prestige are thus diminished, as it is then evident for all to see that they were never even considered.

The Chairman speaks: "In this assemblage, I can see Pa Oluwole, Daddy Joseph and other elders and important figures such as Adio—goldsmith. When the young people came to me and notified that they had designated me chairman, I said to them, 'What about Pa Oluwole? Have you interrogated Pa Joseph? Did Adio—goldsmith decline? Why me'? Ladies and gentlemen, I tell you I was quite surprised. However, here we are. I am Chairman.

"All of us here who have good family background cannot ask for more when your own people honour you with this kind of choice. I am humble."

The demolition of Pa Oluwole, Daddy Joseph and Adio—goldsmith is nearing completion. But the Chairman is not done. He presses on ruthlessly. "The young people were adamant," he says plaintively "and I had no alternative but to accede to their request."

This unconcealed condescension reduces his rivals to rubble.

"I did not even have time to prepare the documents for an opening speech. I just jotted down a few notes which I have somewhere here in my pocket." He fumbles in his pockets and drags out 'brief introductory remarks' to last not a moment longer than half an hour.

It is imperative that the Chairman makes a donation set at a competitive pitch but which no other can beat—or dare. This gift is awarded more as a fee for being honoured with the chairmanship, than a contribution to charity.

I once played m.c. to a dance. When Mr Chairman had concluded his speech, he leaned over and whispered to me that he would contribute £5, but would I kindly announce that he had given £10? And when I raised a quizzical look, he said breezily: "I have to think of my good name, you know."

The Chairman is a romantic figure, an arbiter, a headmaster, a chucker—out, dictator and verbal felon.

Whether his audience likes (or understands) his sense of humour or not, it is incumbent that they raise raucous guffaws of roaring approval everytime he pauses for breath.

Who's prayers are answered, mine or his?

ETIQUETTE

The richness of Nigerian etiquette is embedded in the romance of speech. Politeness is expressed, not performed. Dropping in on friends unexpectedly is the formal thing. Therefore, when a Nigerian prepares his meal, it is in excess, in anticipation of uninvited stomachs which may drop bye. It is very bad etiquette to prepare a meal sufficient just for yourself and family alone, even if you are not expecting guests.

Occasionally, there are accidents when there is not enough for the visitor to join in; but your embarrassed host would never dream of asking you, as the Europeans are wont to do, to "take a chair and have a drink", while he eats on.

Good breeding demands that he profers an invitation. But. . . . . .

YOU ARE NOT INVITED

If your host says:

(a) We are just washing our fingers.
(b) Will you have something to eat?
(c) Have you recently fed?
(d) Join us, although I doubt if you will like this broth.
(e) You meet us in peace.

YOU ARE INVITED

If your host says:

(a) Please sit with us and let us give praise to God.
(b) Your steps have guided you right.
(c) Your prayers are answered.

Even then, it is insufferably impolite to accept an invitation to a meal upon the first offer, or the second, or the third. Keep stalling until your host loses his patience, then accept wearily.

If invited to dinner, it is pertinent to arrive terribly late, for it is bad manners to give your host the impression that you are eager for his meal. You've got to show your host that you too have food in your home and you are doing him a favour by turning up at all.

When you are offered a drink, refuse it right away, even if you need one desperately.

"Will you have a beer?" asks your host. You shake your head vigorously and deny that you need one. "As a matter of fact, I've just had one." This is very polite.

You're lying into his face and he knows it—the price of beer recently went up and you've reverted to palm-wine which is cheaper and has a more stable price.

Your host presses on. You resist, waiting for the right moment to surrender. When your host says, "Well it's always like that. You never drink in my house" and affects to be injured, you say: "Oh, well I certainly don't remember. . ." You then beg him to give you a beer.

Be cautious, however, to choose the psychological moment. Therefore, use your powers of observation and be keen on your host's sensitivity and credulity.

One friend of mine told me his experience in Sierra Leone. It was his third month and he was fed up with eating in hotels. One day he ran into this Creole chap who invited him to his home.

"Will you have a drop of something?" He was asked on arrival.

My friend protested that he couldn't. He had been drinking all day and one more drop of alcohol would knock him out. In fact, my friend had been saving his apetite for that evening when, he thought, he would have his belly's full in good company.

His Creole acquaintance submitted to his protest, poured himself a drink and sat down.

"What's your hotel like?" his host asked after a long pause.

"Oh, quite comfortable," said the Nigerian, trying not to think of the bugs that kept him company.

"Will you stay to dinner?"

"Oh no, I couldn't."

"Why not? Have you fed?"

"Well I knew I was going to be out late, so I had an early meal. Quite full up, thank you very much."

His Creole host went on and had a hearty meal.

And now my friend says all Sierra Leonians are rude people. Foreigners must never take offence if a Nigerian friend promises to call and does so two weeks after the first anniversary of his promise. He's only being polite.

It is not the habit of Nigerians to live to ripe old age. An old man is therefore viewed with something of the awe reserved for a freak. He knows the secret of life. For this reason, an older person is always addressed in the plural, the origin of this probably being that you have to have more than one life to live to old age.

You have a glimpse of Nigerian etiquette in this message from a son to his mother:

"My beloved mothers, it is such a long time since I last heard from you all and I am beginning to wonder if you all have forgotten me. How are Saibu's mothers, are they well? Are their older son well as well?"

The message makes sense—in the singular.

There are no price tags; although there are prices.

improvising, gesticulating and polishing up his accent so that when he does make his speech, he has everyone confounded. People are accustomed to not understanding their Chairman and they will form a most excellent impression if he speaks between clenched teeth.

The Chairman is ushered to the platform after an elaborate introduction which has its set pattern of protocol. It begins with the m.c. seeking attention but is held up in a traffic jam of interruptions as everybody turns to hush-up everybody else.

Protocol demands that the m.c. keeps the name of the Chairman a closely guarded secret until the tail end of the introduction when he may offer it as the highlight of his speech. Although the name has been published in the programme, in handbills and on posters, this stunt is welcomed with joyous approval.

The m.c. says that it is his bounden duty, his responsibility, his pride and pleasure "to introduce our father for this evening's occasion."

"Everyone knows that there cannot be two Chairmen for the same occasion (*cheers*). Therefore, we can only pick one captain for our boat tonight (*prolonged applause*). We all know the man I have in mind but before I call upon him to assume the chair, I will seek your indulgence and his kind permission to digress a little.

"Who is this man who will be our Chairman this evening? He studied London matriculation in Bombay after the war, having retired from the RAF as a full sergeant (*loud ovation*).

"He did not return home, but went to London to seek the golden fleece (*a sigh of admiration permeates the audience*). He struggled on without a town union support or government scholarship until he passed his B.A. and his intermediate LL.B. (*prolonged loud ovation*).

"Since returning home, our august Chairman tonight has been personally responsible for drafting four petitions to

Government concerning the improvement of social amenities in our town in particular and Nigeria in general." (*Standing ovation*).

The Chairman-elect rises and strides purposedly to the platform. He bows solemnly and commences: "Ladies and gentlemen, when I was apprised of the invitation to chairman this occasion, I perceived that there were many better qualified than myself."

The audience is not deeply touched by this humility, although they would sneer if he did not take time off from the main proceedings to humble himself in this manner. Everyone knows that Mr. Chairman is only making the customary opening gambit and that what he really means is that no one present is better qualified to be Chairman than himself.

With calculated insinuation the Chairman launches a sly attack on his social rivals. By insisting that he had only half-heartedly accepted to be Chairman, he unmasks other outstanding figures in the community whose image and prestige are thus diminished, as it is then evident for all to see that they were never even considered.

The Chairman speaks: "In this assemblage, I can see Pa Oluwole, Daddy Joseph and other elders and important figures such as Adio—goldsmith. When the young people came to me and notified that they had designated me chairman, I said to them, 'What about Pa Oluwole? Have you interrogated Pa Joseph? Did Adio—goldsmith decline? Why me'? Ladies and gentlemen, I tell you I was quite surprised. However, here we are. I am Chairman.

"All of us here who have good family background cannot ask for more when your own people honour you with this kind of choice. I am humble."

The demolition of Pa Oluwole, Daddy Joseph and Adio—goldsmith is nearing completion. But the Chairman is not done. He presses on ruthlessly. "The young people were

THE SPIRIT OF COMPROMISE

No Nigerian arrangement is permanent unless that which has been arrived at by negotiated compromise.

This fundamental principle is more than a habit. It is deeply rooted in the way of life. It is a religion. A situation in which normalcy is achieved without compromise is suspect and every effort will be made to disrupt it so that a proper compromise can be worked out to ensure durability.

For example, the Nigerian labour movement once had one central trade union body. It was one which had been obtained by the voluntary association of various labour bodies in the country. This was a terrible state of affairs.

The labour leaders put their heads and hearts together and began a bitter quarrel which split the movement wide open. Then they re-grouped under two central movements—thus achieving a compromise between having a unified labour movement and having diverse mushroom labour movements.

But there was a third movement which could not accept this compromise and broke away. LATER, ALL THREE CENTRAL LABOUR BODIES COMPROMISED IN WHAT THEY CALLED THE "JOINT ACTION COMMITTEE."

Take our politics for another example.

Radical Nigerian political parties of the First Republic were a compromise between trumpeted socialism and actual conservatism; but there were others too which were a compromise between strictly business ventures and group political interest. When they were parties they were not political and when they were political they were not parties.

No other sphere of national activity provides better

opportunity for compromise than when Nigerians agree to arbitration, which in Nigerian parlance means a compromise between settling a dispute and reaching no conclusions.

When a Nigerian is invited to arbitrate, he knows that he will be condemned by both sides if he does not find fault with either side to the dispute—and praise both for their infinite patience, at the same time. Thus, he will lean over backwards to blame the obviously innocent party and pick on a trivial trespass so that he can be seen to have been fair.

The result of this arbitration would then be a compromise between a lasting scar and a fresh wound. The arbitrator's equivocative upbraid of the guilty party is enough to instil a sense of guilt; yet his censure of the innocent party is sufficiently unfair to arouse fresh hostility.

In most parts of the world, a price tag tells you the exact cost of an article on display in a market. Not so in Nigeria.

There are no price tags; although there are prices. Which is a fair compromise between giving goods away and having prices.

What happens is that the market mammy knowing that the correct price of a dozen eggs is five shillings, asks one shilling more; the customer knowing that he should rightly pay five shillings, offers one shilling less.

Then seller and purchaser haggle and haggle and after driving a hard bargain, compromise on five shillings.

Civil servants are also a compromise between incivility and servitude. They are inherently uncivil and economically servile.

The civil servant is underpaid, which makes his service equivalent to servitude. On the other hand, the civil servant takes a razor-sharp tongue to work with him and will snap like the jaws of a crocodile at the least provocation.

Thus, while he is not civil, he is a servant. It is a rare compromise.

The Nigerian diplomat is another romantic compromise.

18

He has been carefully trained to believe that diplomacy is a compromise between a given policy and organised contradictions.

Thus, at international conferences, the Nigerian diplomat has a lot to say, but refrains from saying a lot. Which is most intriguing. This is how it works:

When a Nigerian diplomat rises to make a speech, he only intends to make a "brief clarification"—and not to make a speech. Later, a statement will be issued briefly clarifying the brief clarification which had been briefly stated earlier by the diplomat.

This is solid diplomacy.

Nigeria's entire diplomatic strategy will fall flat on its face if a Nigerian official were to be so undiplomatic as to try to be heard first at an international gathering.

In the First Republic, our diplomats went to great lengths to see that they spoke when everyone else had finished speaking and half the conference were in the tea-room. This was in the great tradition of that technique of diplomacy highly favoured by the political leaders of the period.

It was called the Doctrine of Self-effacement; or the Overseas Policy of Self-concealment.

In practice, it meant that if there was a slim chance to cancel ourselves out at any international affair, we had to snatch it. Most diplomats approved of this and would often tell journalists proudly that Nigeria's successful policy was to hide from exposure.

In other words, our foreign policy was a compromise between being physically present and being effectively absent. Like playing right full-back in a football match, sitting among the spectators.

Every nation in Africa, small or big, was involved in the rat-race to prove that it had arrived. Nigeria's dedicated policy was to avoid participating in this contest which we considered in very bad taste. Although by this indifference we hoped to be recognised as the leading state in Africa.

Marriage is a rich breeding ground for compromise.

In many happy monogamous homes, marriage is a contemplated compromise between bachelorhood and polygamy. This is largely accepted, as marriage itself is understood to be a compromise between promiscuity and public morality.

The Nigerian family is invariably large.

This is understandable, for the Nigerian family includes relations as far distant as the 12th cousin removed. Thus, in fact, the Nigerian family is a compromise between a village and a clan.

*When you summon a Nigerian, saying to him: "Will you please come here a minute?" he will say to you, "I'm coming." In fact, he's not moving. What he really means is that he will join you as soon as he can—which may be ages.

Therefore, his answer is a compromise between outright refusal and rushing over to see you.

NOISE FROM THE SOUL

In the beginning, God created the universe; then He created the moon, the stars and the wild beasts of the forests.

On the sixth day, He created the Nigerian and there was peace. But on the seventh day while God rested, the Nigerian invented noise.

No noise is ever quite like the Nigerian noise. If you were a good student of noise, you would soon find out that the solid, compelling monotony of Nigerian noise is something exciting and companionable; and after a while, that you really begin to miss this regularised, unabated noise, such as when you are temporarily abroad for instance.

A successful European buys a house in the country and spends the greater part of his life seeking solitude and quiet. He climbs mountains and joins a country club distinguished for its silent fun; where members do not speak to one another unless it is absolutely essential, such as when a brooding club-mate is on fire and hasn't noticed it.

In Nigeria you are regarded with suspicion if you seek solitude, climb mountains and have a house in the country.

For years the British tyrant fought a ruthless war against our noise by imposing crippling fines. You could not shout in court premises; you could not raise your own voice in a hospital. You were not even allowed to call out in church to a friend you had not seen for a whole week.

A national resistance was waged against this intolerable attempt to trample our cultural heritage underfoot and history will remember those brave taxi drivers, music shop owners and loudspeaker operators advertising soft drinks, whose noise put

21

Long time no see !

together would cause an earthquake of such force that would sink the British Isles and half of Continental Europe.

When two long-lost English friends meet they are capable of draining their emotions in seven monosyllabic cough-drops: "I say. John Bull, is it not?" Anything further is considered a disgraceful exhibition of emotion.

In Nigeria, when two long-lost friends meet, it takes the strong intervention of friends to part them.

Houses may be blown down, telegraph poles sheared off and a hundred jet fighters dive through the window, they would be blissfully unaware.

The English dictionary describes the word "salute" as: "To greet with words or with a gesture or with a kiss; to greet; to hail; to honour formally by a discharge of cannon. . . . ."

Too true. The Nigerian greeting is a discharge of verbal cannon complete with firing squads and the rattle-tat machine-gun fire of sweet nothings.

The Nigerian is a greatly demonstrative extrovert. That frozen chill of the Englishman's greeting truly offends him and you have to have a sturdy back to endure his hearty thumping. When you meet an old friend shower such affection on him, until the recipient of your fond salutation collapses, either from exhaustion or from the sheer frustration of trying to ward off further courtesy.

A mastering of this full-blooded greeting comes in handy if you wish to repel or thwart the effort of a bailiff arriving to serve ejection notice.

Upon sighting him, dash out and take possession of him around the shoulders and holding tight to him with a death-grip, drag him into your home and turn on the shower:

You (as if to a long-lost brother): "Welcome!"
He (eyes blazing with hostility): "I thank you."
You (warmly): "How?"
He (coldly): "Fine".

Stare him hard in the eyes, daring him to introduce the unpleasant subject of rents and ejection in the face of such overwhelming welcome. He wouldn't dare.

You (*relieved*): "I said to the wife the other day, 'It's a long time since we saw Ojo—bailiff'; and she said 'Oh well, he's always so understanding, times are hard'."

He (*beginning to weaken, but determined to round up the cash herd*): "Well. . . . I suppose . . . actually I called to see . . . ."

You (*jumping hastily to conclusions*): ". . . . to see if we are in good health! God's blessing forever be with you."

It is forbidden in the Nigerian code of conduct to show irritation, to betray the slightest hint of boredom, or to attempt rudely to alter your host's trend of greeting. Flamboyant courtesy, even of the infamous British type, is the privilege of the host, so carry the offensive and nail Ojo—bailiff to your advantage.

You: "So, how are your family?"

"**Fine**".

"Your father?"

"**Fine.**"

"The wife?"

"**Fine.**"

"The kids?"

"**Fine.**"

Eternal silence, then:

"Long time."

"**Yes.**"

"Welcome."

"**Thank you.**"

"How?"

"**Fine.**"

You (*exultant*): "God be praised."

He (*rising wearily*): "I must be on my way."

24

You (*remonstrating but half pushing him to the door*): "What! Already? Just when I was about to order a keg of palm wine?"

At the door, rumple him up a bit as you would your uncle if he were joining the Army and you are his sole heir.

The Nigerian greeting is a benefit performance between two friends competing to impress on-lookers who of the two is more fond of the other.

The history is told of two Nigerians who had not met in 10 years and sighted each other across a busy street one day in London. They spent a couple of minutes beaming recognition, revved up and charged.

The salutation occurred in the middle of the street as the Nigerians wrapped each other in a bear hug, danced a wild jig and threw punches at each other in the back.

It is said that someone called the police, but this is hotly contested. There is a contrary and widely-held view that there was in fact a policeman on the scene. Anyway, what is important is that the Nigerians were arrested and charged with conduct likely to cause a breach of Her Majesty's peace.

THE ART OF GRUMBLING

Nigerians are a nation of good grumblers.

This should not be mistaken for the dull, inarticulate sounds, the humdrum murmurs, the faintly rumbling growls or those cringing complaints with which the word is often associated.

I mean the full-blooded, roaring type, with its high discourtesy and downright incivility.

Grumbling is an art and everyday in the street corners, in market places, large mammies with marathon stamina, lay new records at grumbling.

The right to moan is taken quite seriously and an employer who interrupts a worker at his grumble, has committed an offence worse than the original object of discontent.

There are several methods of grumbling. Usually, it begins with a shrill, piercing hiss above the roar of traffic, followed by a declaration, favourite among which are, "My father, I'm dead!" Or, if the declarant is in a joyous mood, "I am lost!"

Having satisfied himself that he is dead or merely lost, the grumbler would then tackle the subject of his displeasure.

A politician representing a backwoods constituency, knowing that pipe-borne water or electricity for his area would be impracticable for the moment, and who refuses to grumble about that has, by his own tongue silenced his own political future.

Once in the House of Representatives an MP read out 48 postal agencies, four post offices and one public library which he thought could be built for his people. He bought several dozen copies of Hansard and shipped them home. He was re-elected. *Not one of them was built.*

Not all Nigerians have the real talent for grumbling. Many have acquired the poorer kind; others are addicted to the art in the way that marijuana soothes the dope addict. A few grumble professionally and are to be found in newspaper offices.

GUIDE TO NIGERIAN ORATORY

The power of Nigerian oratory is measured by the strength of the speaker's legs. This is not a Nigerian proverb, but it ought to be.

The practised Nigerian orator is verbose, expansive, repetitive. If there are two ways of making a point, one short, the other long, he will plug for the longer route. Because, in the ears of listeners, it is the length of his speech that will determine its substance, its wit, its power, its influence and its effect.

He begins his marathon address with a familiar apology: ". . . I do not intend to waste your time." Then he goes on to do precisely what you expect him to do—waste your time.

Somewhere in the middle of his speech, he will interrupt himself and seek permission to "digress a little." At this point you can nip out to make that long–distance call to Greenland. Because his "little digression" is an entirely new speech and you will be back in time to hear him say: "Now, as I was saying . . . .", at which point he is resuming the speech he abandoned an hour ago.

Choice ingredients necessary to achieve a famous speech in Nigeria:

(a) Elaborate courtesy
(b) Spices of proverbs
(c) Interjection of prayers
(d) Repetition

A sprinkling of logical conclusions is permissible, but not vital.

Nigerian orators are at their best on state occasions, when kolanuts are first split, after a prolonged argument which

29

"Elders, our fathers, our mothers, my brothers, dear sisters, people young and old, neighbours and friends, God bless us all."

usually begins with a warm debate on who is the oldest person present upon whom the honour will fall to say the prayers. But no orator beats the arbitrator introducing proceedings to the settlement of a dispute.

The head of an arbitration resolving a family feud speaks:

"Elders, our fathers, our mothers, my brothers, my dear sisters, people young and old, neighbours and friends—in the spirit of our ancestors, in the name of the warriors who made our people great, I call you all to witness.

"We all know why we are gathered here this late afternoon. They say that it is he whose moustache is on fire, who smells the burning. And this is true because it is the mother whose son has been eaten by a witch who best knows the evils of witchcraft.

"We are gathered here to resolve the unfortunate bitterness that has split our family into factions. It is right that we should intervene, because our forefathers used to say that a house divided among itself cannot stand.

"I regret to observe that some members of our family do not realise how highly our family is held in this community. They do not know that some members of our family are the envy of other people; that there are people today who would like to take away our name. Otherwise, how can a man for whom a fire has been lit by his enemies go and rub oil on himself and lie close to the fire?

"Well, that is the way of youth. Our old men would say that ignorance is the privilege of youth; alertness is the virtue of the old. And proverb has it that it is the man whose barn is full of yams who must watch out for thieves.

"We are going to investigate this quarrel today. We must. When the cockroach hides itself in a basket of beans, it thinks it is safe; but one day that basket will be opened and the cockroach will reveal itself. Likewise, my elders, my mothers, my brothers, my sisters, my people young and old, my neighbours and friends, the cause of this dispute in our family will reveal itself today.

"Parable has it that no matter how deep down you dive into water to eat banana, the skins will surface. After all, is the secret between a man and his wife not revealed at the ninth month?

"Elders, our fathers, our mothers, my brothers, dear sisters, people young and old, neighbours and friends, God bless us all. May the good memory of our ancestors guide us. May the spirit of our ancestors protect us all. May the Great One give us all long life."

At this point the great opening speech is interrupted as everyone turns to shower blessings on everybody around. If there are members of the family absent overseas, their names are summoned to prayer as well.

"Elders, our fathers, our mothers, my brothers, dear sisters, people young and old, neighbours and friends, I appeal to our brothers and sisters to approach this arbitration with a spirit of compromise, because the child who says his mother shall not sleep, shall himself not sleep.

"As for us who are intervening here today, we are going to be fair in this matter, for proverb has it that an elder who is kind to youth will never starve."

This is classic oratory.

When the first complainant is called upon to state the case of his faction, he will be very rude to launch straight into the heart of the matter. In that event, hardly many would listen to him and his case would be doomed.

He must begin with traditional courtesy: "Elders, our fathers, our mothers, my brothers, dear sisters, people young and old, neighbours and friends, as God is my witness, I want to thank our fathers, our mothers, our dear sisters, our young people, our neighbours, who have kindly consented to arbitrate in this matter.

"The crocodile does not shed tears and whatever decision is arrived at here today we shall accept, because after all when the elephant falls dead, who will bear its corpse away?

"Speaking for myself, I am prepared to accept the verdict of our elders. Is it not said that one man cannot battle with a multitude, but that the multitude can cope with any situation?

"There has been trouble in this family, let us admit it. In a market when there's confusion you don't have to tell even a mad man that people are running for safety. Everybody knows that we have been having trouble in our family.

"Yes, our elders say that you don't have to tell a deaf man that war has broken out. Similarly, even pretenders in our midst know that there has been trouble.

"Our forefathers had the saying that the elders of a community are the voice of God. (Pause). Any man or woman present here who says he does not want to reach old age should put his hand up. (No takers; pause). "God bless us all. God give you child—good children who will look after you in your old age; who will honour your name; who will not fall into white man's case."

By now the crowd is almost on its feet as it answers "Amen" to each pause in the complainant's case.

Then—

The other party is called upon to state the case for the defence. Their leader goes through the same routine of protocol. And when he's done, he reverts to parable to emphasise his point. He says:

"That is our case, my dear elders, fathers, mothers, brothers, sisters, friends and neighbours. Perhaps we shall be found to have been in the wrong. I am not dismayed by the possibility. Is it not our elders who say that all dogs eat rubbish but it is the unlucky ones that get caught?

"Oh yes, we shall abide by the decision of our elders and I assure you that this shall not be in the mood of the man who said to his enemy, 'When you bit me in the arse you didn't look at my behind. When I bite you in the nose therefore, why should I look at the mucus in your nostrils?' "

Point by point, speaker after speaker slams home parable after proverb. The idea is to wear out your listeners, because the power of your oratory will be determined by the strength of your endurance.

If your listeners save their sanity and survive you, then you have made a poor speech.

Sometimes, however, a speech is dragging really too long even for the orator. He would interrupt himself with: "What was I saying?" Whereupon everyone would promptly volunteer the link in the broken thread of oratory.

This keeps the audience awake.

THE "DASH"

In the Continent they offer financial reward in gratitude for services rendered.

They tip the taxi driver for giving them a nice ride through a circuitous route to their correct destination; they tip the newstand vendor for risking his health in a cold booth to sell them newspapers. They tip the dainty usherette who guides them through dangerous aisles in a darkened cinema hall; they tip the lift attendant for attending the lift; and if a waiter brings them their change, they tip him for not keeping it to himself.

How simply horrible.

Tipping has become such an important arm of the national economy of certain Continental countries that appreciation is compulsory and experts have worked out a national minimum cash equivalent of saying "thanks old buddy boy." This is arbitrarily pitched at ten per cent, though sometimes variable, such as if the hotelier feels he has sufficiently slaughtered you and his conscience gives him a little tickling.

This barefaced robbery is delicately called "service charge". In fact it is bribery, which is a very dirty word and quite repulsive to the Nigerian, who thinks it is vulgar that good service should be rewarded only *after* the deed is done.

In Nigeria, by the time a waiter brings your change, you are on the verge of calling the police. Hence the origin of "dash" which is a "service charge" preceeding the service.

We have the sweetly quaint custom of expressing gratitude in anticipation of services about to be rendered.

This is called "dash".

Even when a Nigerian negotiates or demands a gift which is

sure to influence his judgment, he does not accept the interpretation that this is "bribe". It is for him not corruption, but merely a fee or the price for doing you a favour. He's not kidding.

Because it is a favour when he does his job. I mean, he might well refuse to attend to you. So, what do you do about that? Go to the boss? Rubbish. The boss probably received a "dash" before employing him.

"Dash" may be offered in solid cash; it may be made out to a recepient in landed property; it may be small change—as long as it is given *before* the service. Which is like paying your bill before you have seen the menu.

Thus, while tipping is reward, the "dash" is an incentive. But if certain evil persons offer it as inducement, accept it with the rational conviction that had you received it *after* and not *before*, it would have been a tip instead of a bribe. Many people have accepted patronage for lesser reasons.

I recommend the "dash". It reduces hostilities to the barest minimum.

THE MOURNING GAME

When a death occurs in Nigeria, the mourning that follows is usually a game of conventional grief played between the bereaved and sympathisers.

The Nigerian attaches equal importance to death as he does to life. If a man dies childless or passes away when still comparatively young, his body is laid to rest without much ado, the theory being that his spirit is evil and had not justified his coming into the world.

But if he departs, to use a Churchillian phrase, after the pub closes, then his family are under strict obligation to mark the event of his death in a merry way. His spirit was good and there is thanks to give to God for sparing him through the high infant mortality rate, past the many deadly diseases of tropical Africa, into old age.

Deeply felt anguish is compulsory for friends who are required to prove openly that they approved of the dearly departed.

Upon the death of a man, the family quickly gather and surrender their life's savings. In certain rural areas hunters are hired, supplied with kegs of gun-powder and told to commence firing their DANE guns for seven days. In the cities where traditional customs have been over-taken by European influence, a "bull dog" amplifier is rented and the latest beat music and highlife records, played to dancing sympathisers.

There are variations to this and you will find slight changes here and there. But cosmopolitan Lagos provides a general picture.

As soon as you are informed that your friend has lost his

father, proceed to his house and register your sympathy at once. Later, at night, repeat your call. You will find a crowd of mourners in the center of the living room, doing their utmost to out-weep the widow. As you stagger into the middle of the floor, let out a fearsome yelp, leap as high as you can spring, crash to the floor, and writhe with paroxyms of torment.

This performance is watched patiently for a while, then you are dragged off the floor before you can monopolise the scene. Appropriately at this point, the widow murmurs sweet gratitude for your show of affliction.

Take leave of her and join the conversation at the far end of the room where sympathisers, out of the widow's ear-shot, are heatedly discussing high market prices, politics and the latest matrimonial scandal in town.

Some time later, a guest mourner for want of anything better to do, will launch into milestones of the deceased's lifetime. Join in.

"Do you remember the day of his return from Burma? How his face lit up when he saw his wife on the quay?" (*Everyone muses dejectedly on that memorable incident.*)

"Are you telling me," resumes another voice, "what about the fond way he used to hold his eldest child when he was a toddler? Such an affectionate father. Such a good man. And didn't they say he left several rented houses behind?"

This eulogy goes on endlessly.

Suddenly, an old woman breaks into a song of lament in which she invokes the spirit of the deceased, and recounts phases of the deceased's life in the way that a priest takes the pulpit to recount the deeds of a dead parishoner who never stepped into church throughout his lifetime, except at harvest time when he came to take part in the raffle.

If the deceased was an inconsequential rogue who had made a nuisance of himself during his lifetime, the old woman takes refuge in dirges sung to his ancestors, as if the deceased had been personally responsible for their feats and glory.

Meanwhile, the widow takes time off to think where she is going to find the money to keep up appearances. Woe-betide her if she does not enter into debts in celebration of her husband's passing. Then you will hear someone comment: "Terrible woman! When her husband died you know that she was so miserly? Would not spend a penny and he left her gold earrings, bangles and bales of damask."

A widow left with a pension by her husband is not only expected to spend the entire money, she is also expected to boast about it.

The story is told of the widow who walked behind her husband's cortege and kept murmuring; "Goodbye darling dearest. I thank you for the two-storey house you built in the market place; the gold necklace you had delivered to me last year; and that hand-woven wrapper made to match the 'agbada' you wore to Asake's naming ceremony..."

Relations who wouldn't give the deceased a drink of water in the middle of the Sahara in his lifetime now turn up with their friends, carrying cartons of beer and demanding attention so everyone can see how much they loved "Cousin Mustafa".

The last mark of respect and affection is established at the graveside by the widow begging to be buried alive with her husband. All loving widows threaten to throw themselves into the yawning pit, but as this is anticipated there are powerful hands ready to restrain them.

One genuinely moved widow forgot her part and was walking away, to the complete astonishment of other mourners. Then near the gates she regained her composure, hurried back to the graveside and called out to everyone to witness that she was willing to make the jump. The mourners trooped back with much relief and duly restrained her.

With the dead laid to rest, the social event now begins proper. The widow picks a special print of cloth which all her

41

relatives and friends purchase from her. She has obtained large bales of this print on credit from a Lebanese textile merchant and she can then re-sell at 100 per cent profit to sympathisers. This is the uniform called "Aso-ebi", sewn to the exact style by more than 300 mourners, which will be worn on the night of the wake-keeping (called "waking" in Nigerian English).

Romance has blossomed for some youthful middle-aged widows at the wake-keeping for their beloved departed.

Three months after the wake, the family attend a thanksging service (sometimes erroneously described as "memorial" service). But it is thanksgiving, because this is the last official rite performed and the cost of putting the old goat to rest has reduced everybody to penury. On the first anniversary of the passing, a "remembrance" service is held.

After that the advertising departments of newspapers take over with their "in memoriam" columns.

THE TELEPHONISTS

The Nigerian telephone operator and the taxi driver have one thing in common. They both drive you round the bend.

If you want to take a long holiday away from your family and friends—and retain their greatest affection, then use the telephone regularly. It won't be long before you are ripe to be put away.

Some ignorant foreigners hold the erroneous view that telephones are a device for transmitting speech over a distance. Well they're wrong.

In fact, a telephone is a gadget for recording silence. It is also an instrument installed in the home or office to relieve boredom. When life becomes monotonous and dull and friends and relations are nice and pleasant, you can obtain a good quarrel and get happily ruffled at very low charges, by merely lifting the receiver and calling the telephone operator.

It is all part of the welfare services provided by a very considerate State which no doubt believes that a regular exchange of insults among its diverse citizens is a good thing for drawing people close.

Unfortunately, not many people appreciate the value of this scheme; in spite of the fact that Government spends large sums annually to ensure that telephones are not in working order and if they are, that telephone operators know the appropriate swear words in vogue.

The aim of every telephone operator is to contradict you. To call you when you do not wish to be called; not to answer when you are calling. To refuse to admit that you have the wrong number; never to put you through to the right number.

Wrong number...? Not on seat . . . ?

For instance:

You: "Is that three-three-six-six-four?"

"This is double-three-double-six four."

You: "May I speak to extension double-nine-seven?"

"Hold on."

Three quarters of an hour later you drop the telephone, wait a few minutes and call 33664 again.

You: "You asked me to hold on for extension 997 and that was the last I heard from you."

"Me? Asked you to hold on? Look at this man! Are you sure you have the right number?"

You: "Is that not double-three-double-six four?"

"This is three-three-six-six-four"

You: "Then it was you I called three-quarter-hour ago."

"Several people have called this morning, how am I supposed to know? Have I met you before?"

You: "Give me extension nine-nine-seven."

"You want extension double-nine-seven? Why didn't you say so in the first place? Hold on."

Five minutes later you tap the telephone impatiently.

"Yes?"

You: "I'm still holding on for extension 997".

"Not on seat."

A telephone at home is a status-symbol in Nigeria.

THE BUREAUCRAT

If the British ever come back—a possibility which is strengthened by the number of Beatles records sold in Nigeria—they will find that among the few institutions they left behind which have survived independence, is bureaucracy.

Bureaucracy is the art of officialdom by officials for the sake of officialdom.

It is also a national ritual performed by everyone with tne slightest advantage of being placed in a position in which he has to perform a function for members of the public.

Let us say you want to buy postal orders worth 15/3d and that you want to register this to your cousin in Niamey, who has written to say that unless you send him this amount readily, he will be thrown out of his university.

You rush to the post office. There is an array of notices above the counter. One reminds you that the design, colour and size of all currency notes have changed five years ago and you're therefore warned that anyone caught immitating the engraving will be severely dealt with.

You turn to the uniformed gentleman at the door and ask politely: "Please can you tell me where to buy postal orders?"

"I'm sorry", says the man in the brown uniform. "I'm a gateman here. Ask the messenger".

He's not being rude. He's only being bureaucratic.

Notwithstanding the fact that post offices are much praised for their bureaucratic efforts the Customs are the most efficient bureaucrats in the land.

You must remember that the aim of every Customs clerk is to make you prove that in spite of his strong suspicions, you are not a smuggler. For this reason very elaborate traps have been carefully set down on paper amid a confusion of expert bureaucratic ambushes.

Many smugglers escape this dragnet, but it is not because our Customs men are dumb. It is because the paper work with which smugglers were once effectively way-laid are not enough today.

Let us say you want to import your dog into Nigeria. They have special forms in which you state the name of your pet, its age, its port of embarkation and most important, its port of disembarkation (the fact that you are filling the form for Lagos, in Lagos, notwithstanding).

When you have satisfied the medical powers that your dog is safe to join the horde of flea-infested mongrels rampaging among the city's dustbins, you would take your permit to the Customs along the Marina, next door.

Here you will fill more forms and be told to take them to Apapa. At Apapa you would be stopped at the gates and asked if you have obtained a permit to enter the port area. You haven't. So you must go to the Ports Authority who will take down all particulars about you, to prevent you committing a felony.

Armed with their permit you can now invade the port area and after a search lasting only two hours, locate the "shed" where a dog is barking.

If you are lucky you will find it is your dog and that all that remains to be done is to fill the right forms at Apapa, bring them to Lagos for approval and take them back to Apapa again, having previously obtained another permit from the Ports Authority to enter the port area.

If you are unlucky, then it is quite possible that your dog has been shipped to Port Harcourt due to a misunderstanding between the ship's bursar and the Customs clerk, disagreeing over the right forms.

What the Government should do is make people fill out Customs forms in Ibadan, discharge their luggage in Kano and see the Immigration in Enugu. It will be most popular, because Nigerians are bureaux crazy.

A friend of mine wished to clear up a knotty point that had arisen as a result of a recent issue of the Government Gazette.

Because it concerned trade regulations, he took his problem to the Ministry of Trade and Industry. He was advised that it was a legal issue; therefore, to see the Ministry of Justice.

There he met a young lawyer who confessed he had had hands in drafting a clause of the regulation in question. The young lawyer advised my friend to go to the third floor and see a senior official who actually compiled the law.

The official on the third floor was very moved that so much interest was being taken in his work. Filled with enthusiasm, he called up the messenger and asked him to tell the clerk on the ground floor to come up. Ten minutes later, the filing clerk arrived and received instructions. Whereupon, he climbed one more flight of steps to obtain the key with which to open the filing cabinet placed on the second floor.

He returned sometime later with the file under his armpit. The senior official studied the file briefly, smiled a smile of satisfaction . . . and then his face paled. "Mr. Diobu", he whispered hoarsely. "I cannot let you have the contents verbatim. It is here all right, but I cannot let you see it."

Mr. Diobu was quite shaken. "Why not?" he asked.

"Because," said the official heavily, "it is confidential."

The official was ashen and very thoughtful as the shock of what he had nearly done passed over him. Then his face lifted and he said brightly, "I know what you can do."

"What?" asked Mr. Diobu eagerly.

"Go to the Ministry of Trade and Industry and apply through them to us. I promise to deal with your matter with utmost urgency."

If you are a German answering a newspaper advertisement for a job with a Nigerian hospital, you're very likely to be asked to address your application through the Nigerian Embassy in Bonn, which will direct it to the Ministry of External Affairs in Lagos. The Foreign Office will pass it on to the Ministry of Health, which will in turn ask the appropriate hospital board of governors for advice.

Since there is a vacancy, the following letter will be addressed to you:

"Dear Sir; Re your application, Job Vacancy—Utorkpo General Hospital.

"I am informed by the board of governors of Utorkpo General Hospital that a vacancy exists in the said hospital.

"Please report at the German Institute for Tropical Diseases hospital, Garmisch, to Dr. Hans Schneider, to whom a copy of this letter is addressed, who will introduce you to our Interviews Panel which is a body set up in co-operation between the Governments of the Federal Republic of West Germany and the Republic of Nigeria, and which have instructions under a separate letter addressed to them from this Ministry, to examine your credentials and certificates and advise us accordingly.

"I am directed to say that your application has been referred to the board of governors of the Utorkpo General Hospital for action."

Very few letters are signed by the appropriate public servant. Therefore, your letter will be attested to by: "Isaac Bolaji, for Acting Deputy Senior Assistant Secretary."

There are four grades of official secrets in the Public Service.

1. URGENT—which means the matter is confidential, otherwise it will not be urgent.

2. CONFIDENTIAL—which means it is not necessarily urgent, but should be confined to the city limits and not told to the provinces.

3. SECRET—more than confidential, but not sufficiently secret to be an absolute secret.

4. TOP SECRET—an absolute secret, which should be known only to the messenger, filing clerk, stenographer, stenographer's maternal aunt who is the head of the Association of Market Women, the Permanent Secretary and the Permanent Secretary's mistress down town.

Moslems have their Koran; Christians have their Bible. The Nigerian public servant has his General Orders.

This massive book of rules tells the good public servant how to behave; how not to behave. How to be himself; how not to be himself. It gives such details as how to obtain a loan to purchase a bicycle and the fact that you may not sign your name on any document in red ink.

The "G.O." as it is fondly called, is the last authority on bureaucracy.

A friend of mine, soon to retire from the Public Service, is threatening to write a book on, "What I know About G.O." Being a good public servant who knows his onions, he has formally asked for the kind permission of his superiors to write his book.

The last time he gleaned the file containing his application, it was in the "pending" tray of his most senior officer who has marked it "B.U. on Mr. Nzeribe's retirement date."

Meanwhile, my friend has been told verbally that as he is still a public servant he cannot rightly write anything about G.O His application will be considered on his retirement. And of course he realises that no one knows to whom authority to grant such permission belongs.

All the same since he is an experienced civil servant; he has been asked to submit a memo through his Higher Executive Officer, advising the Assistant Secretary who will let the Permanent Secretary know through the Senior Assistant Secretary, who it is has such power.

TAXI DRIVERS

An arresting means of communication in Nigeria, is the four-wheeled motorised vehicle which is either a "pleasure car" or "lorry".

Private cars have a township speed limit of 30 m.p.h.; taxi drivers have two speed limits—stop and full ahead.

Private cars are road vehicles; taxis are low-flying groundcraft. The difference between an aeroplane and the Nigerian taxi is that one takes off, the other just fails to take off.

It is believed in some quarters that the speedometer is meant to show the driver how fast he is going; in fact, the speedometer was devised to show the Nigerian taxi driver how fast he's not going.

A taxi driver considers it his obligation to get his fare to his destination in the fastest possible time. This noble intention is, however, conspired against by Police authorities who place their agents strategically in the streets and highways, with the sole aim of thwarting the enthusiasm of long-suffering taxi drivers.

This malicious campaign of the Police efforting to bring order into road usage is carried too far, as far as the taxi driver is concerned.

For example, a spiteful weapon adopted by the authorities is the despotic imposition of "one-way" signs. This often means that the shortest distance between two points is not a straight line, and taxi drivers find this most frustrating.

Happily all round, there are not enough traffic cops to patrol all the streets at the same time and keep a round-the-clock watch on taxi drivers. Which is probably why the Taxi Drivers' Union has never taken the Inspector-General of Police to court.

You've heard of chaps driving on their brakes; you've heard of blokes driving on the clutch; you've never heard of fellows driving on the horn. Our taxi drivers do.

Never take a Nigerian taxi driver's word for it.

If he sticks his right arm out, he does not intend to make a right turn. If he sticks his left arm out, he does not intend to make a left turn. He's only showing the traffic cops that he's got a genuine licence. It is not the custom for taxi drivers to carry genuine driving licences.

'*Easy, mister! We'll catch it at the next airport.*'

Merchant of Death.

THE MAULERS

The most romantic means of travel, which is very popular with the Nigerian, is the mammy-wagon.

This is a converted lorry interspersed with sturdy planks for passengers who sit with their backs to the direction in which they are being transported. This is important, as they must not know what is going on in the driving seat.

Sometimes called the "merchants of death" but better known as "Maulers," all mammy-waggons bear religious, memorial and sometimes bizarre titles, ranging from "Ave Maria," "John F. Kennedy," to "One with God is a Majority;" "Simplicity is a Talent," "Man proposes, God disposes" and the ominous warning: "No telephone to Heaven."

The mammy-waggon driver is a tough, hard-driving expert who chews his day through crates of kolanuts which he believes keep him awake. Never trifle with him.

Every good mammy-waggon driver has been carefully trained:

(a)   Never to be over-taken.

(b)   Never to park in the dark with his tail lights showing.

(c)   To admit passengers on the tail-board.

(d)   Not to give signals.

(e)   To be evasive, devious and dubious. Thus, to halt when he should move on; to move on when he should halt. And not to make up his mind whether he is stopping or moving.

(f)   To abandon his vehicle in the middle of a traffic hold-up and complain earnestly to passing motorists that his petrol tank has failed him.

(g)   Above all to sit half in and half out of his vehicle, with his right arm perpetually on holiday while he maneouvres and meanders through traffic and holds conversation with the front seat passenger at the same time.

During his apprenticeship, the mammy-waggon driver has picked up a high grade of swear words. Never tangle with him.

Travelling in mammy-waggons is the cheapest means of journeying in Nigeria —as a great many people on their way to heaven have found out.

FIFTH ESTATE OF THE REALM

A phenomenon of post-war Africa has been the emergence of the radicalism sweeping the Dark Continent.

In the late forties and early fifties this radicalism found expression in the struggle for independence. Youths, burning with enthusiasm and full of fervour, threw themselves into the nationalist struggle, thereby letting off a great deal of steam.

Today, in the middle of the sixties, another form of radicalism is sweeping the African youth. It takes several forms, varying from country to country. In Nigeria it has blossomed into what is popularly known as the "progressive".

Never underestimate the Nigerian progressive. He's the Fifth Estate of the Realm.

It is not easy to become a Nigerian progressive.

In the first place you have to become an intellectual. Which means that you must acquire a university degree, preferably a general degree, as this will curtial your confinement at the university and leave you free to pursue the other training you need.

All university graduates are intellectuals. Until a few years ago, they were not too many on the scene. But Nigeria now has five universities. Moreover, one of the universities has opened degree courses for disciplines such as domestic science, which it calls "home economics". The resultant girl-progressive graduating from the kitchens of this particular university is not yet an impact, but that should not be long in coming, when more intellectual girls arrive wielding cookery books and the rolling pin.

A study in economics is essential for the intending pro-

gressive, because all Nigerian progressives are "economists", whether they are graduates of physical education or zoology.

But you will never become an intellectual unless you recite from the classics and can quote direct excerpts from the Gallic Wars.

You can, if you're reasonably smart, get away with occasional interjections of legal and medical terms in your speech. Such as: "I was telling the wife yesterday that though she'd heard of my failings from her friends, she has not proved a *prima facie* case.

"So I stood there rooted to the ground and insisted that it was *non sequitur* for her to assume that posture of thought. And then to my surprise she began to sneeze and I knew, even before calling the doctor that she had an attack of the *filtrable virus* in the *mucous membrane*. That's sore throat you know."

From the earliest times, you would learn that to win attention, you must begin every sentence with: "As Shakespeare said . . ."

Or, you might say: "It's extraordinary. I'm quite flabberwhelmed and overgasted."

But the utmost essential is the ability to put yourself across unintelligibly. This begins with learning a few tricks employed by other Nigerians who have studied in Oxford and have acquired the Nigerian version of Oxford accent.

In order to have a good grounding of Oxford accent, you should practice every morning before the mirror. At these sessions always hold a tea spoon between your teeth and stuff your nostrils with cotton wool, so that when you speak, it would seem that your voice has been transmitted through a can of water.

The more confusing you are, the higher is your intellect and the greater your esteem in the opinion of newspaper editors who are the sole determiners of the "economist" and therefore the progressive.

Their judgment is summary and once they declare you an "economist" no power on earth can assert the contrary.

It is important—no, vital—that your clothes are carved by carpenters who specialise in ill-fitting designs. Furthermore, that the material used is one that attracts dirt and easily reveals squalor.

You may become an intellectual; you may become an economist. You may become many things; but your progressive colleagues will banish you to the lower orders or even repudiate you totally, if you do not grow a beard.

Having settled the scholarship and sartorial disguise, the pupil progressive should start a pen friendship with the Press and express outrageous platitudes.

Some progressives have had their careers abruptly halted at this stage for proclaiming ideas and ideologies dangerous to the well-being and good order of the State.

Which just goes to prove the grouse of the progressive— that there are still too many reactionaries around in this part of the world. Happily the number of martyr-progressives immortalised this way is negligible and progressives can generally operate without too much interference.

All good progressives are fanatically opposed to dictatorial rule at home. But the good progressive must sympathise with, understand and defend the need for authoritarian rule elsewhere. Provided such rule denies its citizens freedom and liberty in the name of Socialism.

All good progressives despise America and approve of democracy. They extol Russia and disapprove of communism. They oppose the war in Vietnam; the International Labour Organisation; Moise Tshombe; The United Nations; the European Common Market and NATO.

They are devoted to African unity; modern jazz; modern art; Negritude.

Party politics is taboo.

In fact, the progressive must renounce all political parties, declare his conviction that, "Nigerian unity can only be achieved by adopting progressive policies of the Marxian-Socialist concept, which has revolutionised the fate of millions of proletariats once held in bondage by the Czarist bourgeoisie in the agrarian Soviets."

All good progressives are devoted champions of the working class. For this reason, they do not use short words. They are profoundly philosophical as well.

Sample statement: "The orientation of our socio-economic system has engendered the capitalist class into reckless politico-economic adventures in the orbital sphere of neo-colonialists and imperialists".

The progressive is a non-conformist, although you would insult him deeply if you suggested that he is an atheist.

I once heard a progressive postulate that "atheism is a void, an emptiness activated by a philosophical and psychological vacuum. The non-conformist," he said, "is a free-thinker who rejects the ceremonial and trappings attached to conventional Christian worship."

The Nigerian progressive influences the minds of newspaper readers through his "Letters to the Editor" column. He is not a communist, not a fascist, not an anarchist, not a nihilist, but a Socialist".

Basically all progressives are opposed to parliamentary democracy of the Westminster type because it is a Western capitalist ruse to perpetuate economic domination of Africa and extend British political imperialism indefinitely in Nigeria.

The experienced progressive is contemptuous of right and sympathetic to wrong. Which is not as twisted as you may think. For there is often so much wrong with right and such a lot of right in wrong.

Anything a progressive does not genuinely understand is

obviously upper class and oppressive.

No progressive of repute knows the artists of his own country. If, however, through sheer accident, he knows who Ben Enwonwu is, then he is permitted to discuss his works only in the light of the examples of Rembrandt, Van Gough, Michelangelo and their famous achievements.

The teachings of all-time intellectual pillars such as Socrates and the philosophy of Plato are at his finger tips, so don't tempt him.

Occasionally, the progressive accepts invitation to a cocktail party where he is able to put the Americans to fright and frustrate the Russians at the same time.

The United States, he will insist, is spying on Nigeria through the Peace Corps. The USAID programme is another example of neo-imperialist economic domination.

Americans cannot stand this kind of probing and the average American diplomat will take flight at once leaving the progressive more convinced than ever that there is much truth in what he has just disclosed to the diplomat about his Government's vile intrigues.

The Russians, who seem to claim the friendship of the progressive as of right soon find out that they are wrong. When confronted by the progressive the discussion would trail off to the virtues of Chinese ideological stand—a stand which the Russians can't stand.

Visitors who treat the progressive with fleeting levity do not know what they miss. If they would only take a closer look, they would find that there is something colourful about the progressive which has delighted adoring Nigerians for a long time.

For example, no other section of the community has had as many conflicts with the authorities as have the progressives who clearly have no ambitions for power and only would like to take office away from the successive authorities.

For those who wish to converse with a progressive and be understood by him, the following vocabulary is compulsory:

Word	Meaning
Neo-colonialist	Foreign investor
Capitalist	Executive employee
Democratic	Authoritarian
Fascism	Legality
Progressive	Dissenter

In Nigeria the forces of public opinion are divided into two—between the politicians and the progressives, with the public trying hard to get in a word.

SEX

Marriage they say is an institution; sex is incidental.

In Nigeria, sex is an institution and marriage is an incidence.

The ambition of most Nigerian girls is to be the last love of a man. The demand of all Nigerian men is to be the first love of a girl.

The Nigerian is a great lover. If he has a mistress, in spite of a monogamous marriage, everyone will respect it, as long as the woman herself respects the relationship by unquestionable loyalty. This is considered exemplary discipline and evidence of sincerity.

Should she bestow her favours on other men, she will be denounced and her relationship with her lover becomes a dirty affair. For the difference between a healthy relationship and debauchery is in the mistress's loyalty and not in the marital status of the male partner.

Hence, a Nigerian magistrate once said that "illegitimacy is a European concept".

Yet sex is sacred.

It is never talked about in public.

The Englishman considers himself ravingly sexy when he takes his girl in a dark alley and kisses her. In America they have to have "purple hearts" to look a girl in the face a second time.

What the Nigerian needs is not idyllic retreats or "pep pills" to achieve ecstatict romance. He needs tranquilisers.

PATIENCE AFORETHOUGHT

Nigerians are profoundly proud of their patience and you can win him to life-long friendship if you say to a Nigerian that you are grateful for his *patient* understanding.

This monumental patience reveals itself in his phlegmatic nature.

There are few nations in the world where man and the clock have reached amicable settlement. Nigeria is one of them.

Foreigners are often astonished that the Nigerian is completely indifferent to the pressure of time. The secret of this success lies in a gentleman's understanding, whereby each respects the other's province.

If a Nigerian is late for an appointment he takes it with a sporting calm on the cheerful grounds that Time beat him to it this time.

The mistaken impression is abroad that the Nigerian is unambitious and that his cool reserve for Time is evidence of laziness. Wrong. It is simply a matter of letting Time race with time—with the Nigerian as an unperturbed by-stander. As the Nigerian often says, "The clock did not invent man." Give this thought. It is deeply philosophical.

National holidays aside, nothing thrills the Nigerian and cements him in spirit with a fellow Nigerian faster than the unanimous disregard for Father Time. Should Time conspire against him, his countrymen will stand with him to the end against the common enemy.

You invite a Nigerian to dinner for 8 p.m. and he has not turned up at 9 p.m. Do not give up and begin to eat. He is sure to turn up at 9.30 p.m. the next day.

If you don't wait, next day he will complain to a colleague in the office: "Do you know he couldn't even wait". His friend will mark you down as a potential enemy. In many parts of the world, life is a mortal combat between man and ruthless Father Clock, with Father Clock leading by a neck. The implacable resolve of man to battle to the bitter end with time does not attract the Nigerian.

He surrendered a long way back.

Hot tip for the foreigner in a hurry: Instant coffee takes only half an hour to brew in Nigeria. (I don't know if that is original.)

THE COMMON TONGUE

The trouble with the English language is that it is no longer English.

It is the common language of the Ghanaians who are no more English than Chiang Kaishek is Russian. It is the official tongue of the Indians who out-number the British ten to one.

When Nigerians are gathered in mixed tribes, English is the patriotic vehicle of communication.

Although it is not considered bad manners if two members of a Nigerian tribe converse all evening at a party in their tribal language, even though a dozen foreigners are present, it is very bad manners if two Nigerians of the same tribe speak in their native tongue, when a third Nigerian from another tribe is present. At such times you will hear people say: "These tribalists! They won't speak English!"

Such is the passion for the English language that a child will not obtain the all-important West African Schools Certificate if he fails in English.

A Nigerian who writes fluent Arabic and has acquired a command of the French Language in Chad Republic is still not educated, until he can speak and write English as She is spoke.

Other European languages are held suspect. But the French language is held in contempt.

We acquired this judgment from the British.

During British colonial rule you would impress no one if you studied French in school, for no good schools taught French. All good schools taught Latin.

Until this day, if you want to be extremely funny, you say:

67

"parllez vous Francaise?" Your sense of humour will be appreciated for ten days.

When I was with Nigerian troops in the Congo at the height of the troubles and in the thick of the unrest in Katanga, you would relieve the day's tension if you burst into a room and declared: "Merci Bukavu!"

This was considered most humourous.

But the joke was not complete until someone had added: "Il ne par de Manono" That always brought the roof down.

The prefix of the French de before a name has a special significance.

On the one hand it is a jibe at the French, which every sophisticated Nigerian must applaud. On the other hand, it is a mark of endearment. Lastly, it denotes respect and appreciation.

Thus, if you find me funny, you would call out to me: "De Peter!" But if you thought of me as an irretrievable nincompoop, you still said: "De Peter!"

Suppose, however, you are a man of great academic distinction? You would change your name among your friends immediately on being awarded an honourary doctorate, to "Dr. de Kajola!"

Experts are puzzled why the French language has not gained widespread recognition in spite of the removal of direct British influence in the matter. Some say it is because there are not enough French teachers. I think not.

The real reason is that French has always been and has remained the language of the menu card. It is a fact that most restaurants are owned by Lebanese proprietors who, as everyone knows, speak terrible English. Hence they obtain sanctuary in French.

It is this combination of being associated with kitchen language and the fact that only people who speak bad English have good French, that has harmed the French language in Nigeria.

THE LAGOSIAN

There is a popular Nigerian saying that to go to Lagos from your home village is no difficulty; it is to return that is war.

This is very true.

But you can never become a true Nigerian until you have passed through the grill, come to Lagos, or, at the very least, aspire to come to Lagos.

There are 55.6 million people in Nigeria, but only 1.2 million live in and around Lagos. This anomaly is being rapidly rectified by patriotic Nigerians who flood into Lagos with every intention of returning home eventually but without much hope of doing so.

Like David Whittington's London, the streets of Lagos are paved with solid gold. Therefore, the economic structure of the City is clearly divided into two categories—those who own the mines and those who work the mines all their lives.

What is unique about Lagos is that both groups live lives which are not far apart. Let me explain.

Until recently, most wealthy men in Lagos lived in the largest slums. The poor also lived in slums, except that their slums were smaller. Then the Government stepped in and said: "You fellows can't live in this jumble junk fashion, let's have modern slums."

And it came to pass that whole families were herded out to the open plains of Surulere where the Lagos Executive Development Board built a housing estate which were tiny match-box bungalows—but much better slums.

The rich were envious. They piled pressure on the LEDB and complained that they were being cheated. The LEDB

'Say, can I have a couple of thousand quids there?...
I've run out of ready cash.'

understood and made concessions of land, also in Surulere.

Today the rich and poor live in the proudest slums. Thus, once again, Lagos has remained a democracy.

If you live in the provinces and you want to become a Lagosian, what you have to do is take a mammy-waggon ride to the capital. That's all.

You do not need the previous assurance of a job. Everybody in Lagos is employed. If you do not join the mass of domestic servants, you can always run your own private protection club on the premises of hotels, restaurants and night clubs, for car owners whose headlamps will be stolen, tyres deflated or whose cars will be made totally immobile if they do not see the good sense in becoming your clients.

At the very worst you can make a job of standing in queues at the Ministry of Labour. Many Lagosians live an honest life standing in Labour Exchange queues.

You must remember that there are 55 million other Nigerians conspiring against you, because at the present rate of migration, eventually all Nigerians will come to live in Lagos.

Whether you are assured of accommodation or not, it is of no consequence. There is always room under the Carter Bridge. Some Lagosians live there.

An American parent once said to his boy: "Son, education is very important. You either have it so you can employ other people; or you don't have it and employ those who have."

In Lagos, you may have education, but you may not have it. There's always someone around who has it and who will use it to your advantage. All you need is brains.

Get smart.

For instance, if you want to raise a loan in the bank, it is quite easy. Most successful men in Lagos are rich not for the size of their savings, but for the load of overdraft they carry.

To raise a loan, go out and borrow rich robes. Bank managers are always highly impressed by borrowers who dress up richly. Be scrupulously careful not to give the impression that you need the money. Your bank manager will be deeply impressed. If you dress to show that you need the money, you are sure to be thrown out.

Be loud and clear in speech. Say to him confidently: "Say, can I have a couple of thousand quids there? I'm temporarily out of pocket. I've run out of ready cash." Your account will be overdrafted at once.

But if you are daft and you say: "Please, please, can I have five hundred pounds urgently· I'm desperate!" The commissionaire will throttle you.

Having raised a loan, proceed to establish a petty trading business. Do not invest your entire loan in the business. This would be foolish. You must realise that you are at once a successful businessman by virtue of your overdraft. You must realise too that you need a car, a large rented house in the deepest slums—and an extra wife.

Acquire a luscious girl friend whose leading boy friend has contacts in the Civil Service, the Police and the Prisons. Make as many friends as you can on your way up because you will need them on your way down.

Now, please take my word for it that every faithful girl friend wants her lover to succeed. Which means that she must show that he is succeeding. There's nothing like a show of success to promote a business. She would have to buy rich damask, carry craters of gold bullion around the neck. You must co-operate. Be generous.

All good girl friends love money, having boy friends, juju music, highlife music, sex and making babies—in that order.

You can become a Lagosian, but you cannot become a successful Lagosian unless you give parties regularly. Take advantage of the slightest opportunity to give a party. Such as: When your distant cousin whom you never knew dies in

Hong Kong after 20 years of self-exile, the cause of which you knew not.

When it is the 42nd anniversary of the death of your wife's half sister's great-aunt.

When your third wife has her seventh baby.

When you are courting a new mistress.

When your bank manager is going on vacation.

When you have obtained a new overdraft.

When you buy an old car.

Get down to the business of being a "typical Lagos man."

In the evening when you are making the rounds of your various wives, it is most irritating to find provincial drivers clustering the roads and generally showing that they do not know how to use a car in congested traffic. You have an obligation to show them what to do in Lagos. You can tell provincial drivers by their car number plates and the way they behave as if traffic regulations are meant to be obeyed. Be mean and contemptible with these upstarts.

You have a third party insurance policy which is slightly out of date. Take advantage of it.

Slam your fist on the horn ring, hold on tight to the steering wheel with your left hand. Accelerate. Just as you are cruising past this rustic driver from outer space at a considerate 60 m.p.h., stick out your head and cry out: "Bah! bush man. Have you a learner's permit?"

If he puts out his ugly snout and answers back, halt right in front of him and, to use an American expression, make a federal case of it.   (Do not forget to signal *after* you have come to a complete stop.)

That will put him in his place.

Every successful Lagosian endeavours to visit his home town periodically. You must remember that your home-town folks look up to you for example.

On arrival, address your grandmother in Queen's English.

If she doesn't understand you, condescend to pidgin English (called "broken") and if she still doesn't understand you, get an interpreter. Your village will marvel how you have completely lost your tribal language in Lagos.

You can't escape holding a party which must be expensive and quite lavish. You are also entitled to forget the names of your life-long friends, although it is permissible that you vaguely remember their faces. Snap your fingers repeatedly and ask your closest cousin who they are.

Everyone will be suitably impressed.

When it is your turn to speak, begin each sentence with: "When I was in Lagos. . . ." This is very effective in places like Maiduguri where they have heard that Lagos is a South Sea island.

At the end of your stint at home, you will have to return to Lagos, where your accumulated bills are waiting and where debt collectors have been keeping a close watch on your door.

Take heart.

If they send you to prison most Lagosians will sympathise with you and blame the Government.

They too are in the same boat.

FOREIGNERS

There are two consignments of foreigners in Nigeria:

    (a) The Expatriate

    (b) The "Syrian"

Expatriates are people who have white skins; live in reservations; have cooks, stewards and one wife; tell Nigerians what to do, but never how to do it; tell visiting journalists all the latest scandals in high places; assure Nigerians that all is well; play golf; do not speak above a hush; do not speak for hours; will do anything for a dog; squeamish about sex; have helped to re-populate with off-springs, aided and abetted by mistresses, the Rivers areas of Nigeria which were depopulated in the last century by their forebears. All expatriates are called Europeans. They include Americans, Canadians, Frenchmen, Paraguayans, British, Czechs and Germans.

"Syrians" are people with pink skins, who run sophisticated market stalls; stand between the Nigerian petty trader and the Japanese textile manufacturer; people who have trees in their back yards from which money grows over-night; who marry their first cousins; do not marry Nigerian girls; roll their "r"s.

"Syrians" are the Arabs, Chinese, Indians and Outer Mongolians. They are called "Cora", because they made their fortune selling coral beads in the old days. (*The Lebanese do not like to be called Syrians. A pity. They have so much in common*).

To be a good foreigner, you must stay an alien. Nigerians are immensely hospitable to foreigners. They especially like foreigners who know their place as aliens and keep it.

All aliens are popular, who can laugh at themselves when the Nigerian pokes fun at them. It proves that they are good at

There are two consignments of foreigners in Nigeria:
(a) The Expatriate
(b) The "Syrian"

Expatriates are people who have white skins; live in reservations; have cooks, stewards and a wife; tell Nigerians what to do, but never how to do it; tell visiting journalists all the latest scandals in high places; assure Nigerians that all is well; play golf; do not speak above a whisper; do not speak for hours; will do anything for a dog; squeamish about ......; have helped to re-populate whole off-spring ...... and abetted by mistresses, the Rivers areas of Nigeria which were depopulated in the last century by their forebears. All expatriates are called Europeans. They include Americans, Canadians, Frenchmen, Paraguayans, British, Czechs and Germans.

"Syrians" are people with pink skins, who run sophisticated market stalls; stand between the Nigerian petty trader and the Japanese textile manufacturer; supply who have trees in their back yards ...... money over-night; who marry their ...... marry Nigerian girls; roll their "r"'s. "Syrians" are the Arabs, Chinese, Indians and Outer Mongolians. Those are called "Cora" because they made their fortune selling ...... coloured glass beads. (The Lebanese do not like to be called Syrians, but they have too much in common).

To be a good foreigner you must stay an alien. Nigerians are immensely hospitable to foreigners. They especially like foreigners who know their place ...... and keep it.

All aliens ...... distinguish ...... an language ...... themselves when the Nigerian ...... point that they are good at heart. All aliens are unpopular, who poke fun at Nigerians. It shows they are evil at heart, probably even Negrophobists.

All foreigners are held personally responsible for the actions of their Governments at home.

An alien is the foreigner who refuses to become a Nigerian.

'Wonder what they feed to their dogs...

'Wonder what they feed to their dogs...

HUMOUR

The Nigerian sense of humour can be beautifully caustic.

It takes the form of robust impertinence, finished in unsophisticated over-statement. You might say that it is mid-way between the subtle wit of English humour and the artless naivety of the American comic.

It also takes the form of the isolent practical joker.

An expatriate acquaintance of mine was told the story of the Nigerian student who went into a London restaurant and ordered a whole roast chicken. When the Nigerian saw the bill, he was aghast. At home a roast chicken would cost 6/- or less and here he was paying 18/-. He decided he had to do justice to his extravagance and was noisily breaking the bones between his teeth and sucking at the marrows, when an English gentleman presiding over a cup of chocolate ice-cream on the next table, asked him icily what they fed to their dogs in Nigeria.

"Chocolate", answered the Nigerian.

My expatriate friend thought it was quite a funny story and took the liberty to repeat it to some Nigerians a few weeks later at a cocktail party. Most of his audience had heard it before, but they politely refrained from interrupting him. Unfortunately, the European did not recall the retort of the Nigerian and halted at the point where the English man asked his question. Which was still funny, but not a ripple of laughter greeted the story. His audience did not think it was funny that the joke rested on the Nigerian.

The Nigerian ribs himself with self-inflicted humour, but outsiders are not welcome to lay him on the anvil of his own Joke-parlour.